THE HOW AND WHY WONDER® BOOK OF
NORTH AMERICAN INDIANS

Written by FELIX SUTTON
Illustrated by LEONARD VOSBURGH
Editorial Production: DONALD D. WOLF

Edited under the supervision of
Dr. Paul E. Blackwood, Washington, D. C.

Text and illustrations approved by
Oakes A. White, Brooklyn Children's Museum, Brooklyn, New York

PRICE/STERN/SLOAN
Publishers, Inc., Los Angeles
1983

Introduction

The American Indians are an ancient people with a long and noble history. Their many tribes inhabited most of this continent thousands of years before European explorers set foot on it. This *How and Why Wonder® Book of North American Indians* tells their story. The cultures and customs that grew out of how they adapted to their environment are fascinating and exciting.

The Indian's life, however, was irrevocably changed when the white man began his endless thrust past the frontier to eventually occupy almost all the territory once possessed by the Indians.

This book is both history and drama — history in its faithful account of events, and drama in its portrayal of human suffering. What can we learn from this moving chronicle for the present and future? Are there any clues here which will help people with different racial and cultural heritages, but with the same human nature, to resolve their conflicts peacefully?

Look for such enlightenment in the *How and Why Wonder® Book of North American Indians,* for it is to be found. Individually, and in groups, we must evaluate this guidance as we seek ways of achieving a richer life of freedom for all in a world where many groups with different backgrounds, but with common human needs, live side by side.

Paul E. Blackwood

Dr. Blackwood is a professional employee in the U. S. Office of Education. This book was edited by him in his private capacity and no official support or endorsement by the Office of Education is intended or should be inferred.

ISBN: 0-8431-4254-5

Library of Congress Catalog Card Number 65-13787

How and Why Wonder® Books is a trademark of Price/Stern/Sloan Publishers, Inc.

Contents

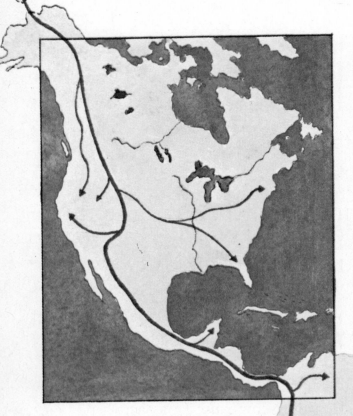

The first American settlers were primitive Asiatic peoples who, thousands of years ago, came from Siberia to Alaska across what is today the Bering Strait. This fact is quite generally accepted although there are scientists who subscribe to the theory that, at times in the geological past, there was a land bridge between Siberia and Alaska over which the Asian migrants wandered; others believe that they came during the season the Strait is frozen over; and a third group contends that they came in primitive boats, making use of the Big Diomede (Russian) and the Little Diomede (American), as steppingstone islands, which cut the total distance of 60 miles sea crossing to only 25 miles at the most. The American Indians, the descendants of these original immigrants, were long established when the first Europeans arrived. The map shows the migration routes of these first arrivals, whose main stream went from Siberia, over North and Central America to South America, with minor side migrations, within what is today's United States.

Traces of the Folsom man of about 10,000 years ago were found in the Southwest. With their primitive weapons, these early ancestors of the American Indians hunted mammoths, giant bisons, and other species of animals now extinct on the continent.

The First Indians

Where did they come from?

Try to picture our country as it was twenty-five thousand years ago. The land looked as it does today — high snow-capped mountains, broad grassy plains, vast expanses of heavy forests, and lazy rivers meandering between banks overgrown with willows and sycamores.

Many of the animals, too, were the same as you would see in the wilds of present-day America—deer, bears, buffaloes, beavers, rabbits and squirrels. But there were also herds of camels and wild horses, and strange creatures that have long since vanished from the face of the earth — saber-tooth tigers, giant

sloths, and gigantic long-haired elephants called mammoths.

One thing, however, was missing. In all the length and breadth of the Western Hemisphere, there was not a single human being. Mankind was unknown. The wild beasts had all this magnificent land to themselves.

Then, on one historic day, most anthropologists agree, a band of Asiatic hunters came from Siberia to Alaska. They had probably been chasing polar bears, walruses, or seals. In any case, they kept going south, making their camp each night when darkness fell in a shallow cave, if possible, or under a protective outcropping of rock. They wore garments made of fur, and carried stone hatchets and stone-tipped spears. They had shaggy hunting dogs that resembled wolves. They made their cooking fires by rubbing dry sticks together.

As the centuries passed on in that long-ago age, other groups of nomadic hunters followed them. In time, the trickle developed into a slow but steady flow of people migrating down through the ridges of the Canadian Rockies into what is now the northwestern United States. Wherever these wanderers went, some settled down and remained. But the more adventurous ones kept moving.

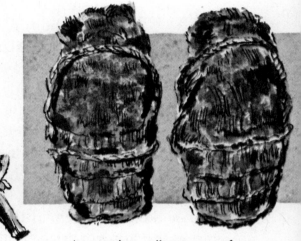

Among the earliest traces of man in North America are these square-toed sandals of shredded sagebrush. Found in a cave in Oregon, they are believed to be 9000 years old.

Found in the early 1930's in a cave in the Grand Canyon in Arizona, this twig deer is about 3000 years old. Scientists believe that it was used as a fetish for a successful hunt.

Primitive Stone Age spear points are among the many relics we have found to date of the early inhabitants of North America.

Some fanned out eastward to the Great Lakes and to the Atlantic Coast. Others went south into Mexico and into Central America. And in a few thousand years — only a few ticks of the clock of geological time — two continents became inhabited by the American Indian.

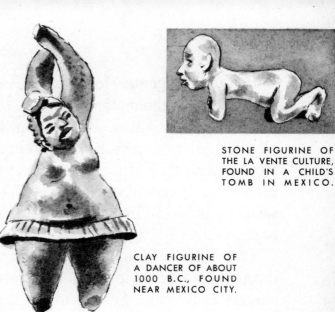

STONE FIGURINE OF THE LA VENTE CULTURE, FOUND IN A CHILD'S TOMB IN MEXICO.

CLAY FIGURINE OF A DANCER OF ABOUT 1000 B.C., FOUND NEAR MEXICO CITY.

How can we trace the Indian migration?

These first Americans left a record of their migrations and history behind them in piles of stones and bones. In caves in Oregon, Colorado, Arizona, Texas, and Mexico, archaeologists have found Indian weapons, crude carvings, the bones of the animals on which Indians fed, and the bones of Indian dead. They left stone arrowheads, spearheads, and cooking pots behind them, and in rare cases, stores of dried grain that have

been miraculously preserved over the centuries. Charcoals have been found from their long-dead fires, and the pictures which they painted are still on the walls of their now-deserted caves.

Scientists have been able to determine the original dates of these relics by what is known as the "Carbon 14" method. This is a recently discovered radioactive measuring process which

The Incas of Peru, Aztecs of Mexico, Mayas of Guatemala, and other Mexican, South and Central American Indians were much more advanced than the North American Indians. Buildings such as this Mayan temple-pyramid show the extent of their culture.

INCA GOLD ORNAMENT, FOUND IN COLOMBIA, WAS MADE BEFORE THE BIRTH OF CHRIST.

INCA CLOTH DOLL, FOUND IN PERU, IS ABOUT 500 YEARS OLD.

AZTEC SACRIFICIAL KNIVES WITH BLADES MADE OUT OF OBSIDIAN.

can establish the age of ancient bones, stones, woods, and other materials within a give-or-take period of a few hundred years. We can be fairly certain that, during the ten thousand or so years which followed the first migration of man into the New World, the human race was established throughout most of North America, Central America, and as far down through South America as the southernmost tip of Chile.

This book is about only the Indian tribes of the continental United States, Canada, and Alaska. A separate account of the Indians of Mexico, Central America, and South America will be given in the future.

How did the Indians get their name? When Christopher Columbus made his famous voyage in 1492, he was searching for a short cut to India. He had no idea that he had accidentally stumbled upon two great continents that lay in the Western Hemisphere between Europe and Asia. He instead believed that he had made a landing on an island in the East Indies. Therefore, in his report to the Spanish Crown, he referred to the natives of the land he had discovered as "Indians." And even though the true "Indians," the natives of India, lived half a world farther west, the name remained in use.

The Indian People

In the thousands of years between the first migrations to the New World and Columbus's discovery of it, the American Indians developed ways of life unique in the world. It is estimated that by 1492 there were about thirteen million individuals living in North and South America. Of these, about a million were scattered through what is now the United States.

The North American Indians were by no means united as one people. They were divided into about five hundred tribes; and these tribes, in turn, were

To send messages to more distant places, the American Indians used smoke signals.

further separated into clans and societies. Some tribes had thousands of members, and roamed over large woodland or plain areas. Others consisted of only a few dozen and rarely ventured outside a secluded area.

While many tribes lived in peace, others fought against each other as deadly enemies. Collecting the scalps of rival tribesmen and then carrying off their women and children as slaves was the accepted way for a young warrior to prove his manhood and become a full-fledged brave.

There were just about as many Indian languages and dialects, too, as there were Indian tribes. Often, a tribe living in one valley could not understand the language of a tribe that lived in another valley which might be only a few miles away. To overcome this communication barrier to a certain extent, the Indians developed a crude sign language —a series of gestures with arms, hands, and fingers — which managed to convey simple meanings. Language experts can find few, if any, resemblances between the various Indian languages and those of the Old World, although certain tribes of the Northwest use some high-pitched, clicking sounds that are faintly reminiscent of Chinese. This probably dates back through the mists

What languages did Indians speak?

of antiquity to the Indians' primeval origin in Asia.

(During World War II, American soldiers who were members of Indian tribes, notably Navahos and Apaches, transmitted and received radio messages at and near the front lines. Their languages could not be translated by linguistic experts in either the Japanese or German armies.)

For the most part, Indian languages are melodious and pleasant to the ear. Their style is eloquent, full of fine phrases and involved descriptions. Many Indian words have become part of our modern American English, as for instance, *toboggan*, from the Algonquin; and from the same source, *arakun*, which has become *raccoon*. Many town and city names derived from Indian languages — Pocatello, Sahale and Thoe, for instance — and so did many names of states and rivers, such as Mississippi and Susquehanna.

How did the Indians live? The Indian was first and foremost a hunter. At some point during the long centuries of his primeval history, he had learned the secret of the bow and arrow. This was a revolutionary improvement over the heavy spear, which was effective only for short-range work. The bow and arrow made it easier for him to kill the deer and buffalo he depended on for his food.

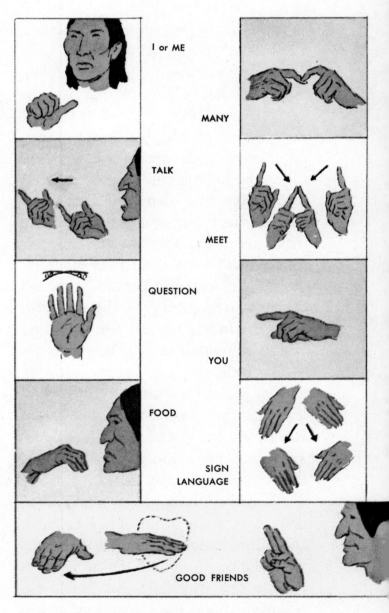

To overcome their communication barrier at least to a certain extent, the Indians developed a crude sign language. Try to make a sentence with the few examples we give here.

He caught small game like rabbits, squirrels, and birds in snares woven of grass and reeds. He netted fish in traps made from tamarack roots or willow branches, or caught them on hooks carved from small pieces of bone.

The skins of wild animals provided clothing for him, and in some cases, the material for his tents and huts. From the sinews, he made sewing threads for moccasins and clothes, fishing lines, and strings for his bows.

Although he was primarily a hunter, the Indian became a farmer, as well. And in becoming so, he developed many of the vegetables that we eat nearly every day.

This was obviously a long, drawn-out process, and it probably began with the gathering of wild vegetables and seeds from the marshes and forest glades. When plants particularly pleased them, the Indians must have encouraged growth by weeding away other undesirable plants, and perhaps loosened the soil to help them grow. By such slow steps, the Indian farmers began eventually to cultivate domestic crops.

The Indians developed corn from a wild grass into a fruitful grain, America's number one food crop today. Beans, squash, pumpkins, and potatoes are also modern food staples originated by the Indians. One of their favorite dishes was a mixture of corn and beans cooked in meat broth. They called it succotash, and we still call it that when we find it on our dinner tables.

Wild rice, which grows in the marsh country around the Great Lakes, was another agricultural development of the Indians. Today it is a luxury food, and fairly expensive; it has never been turned into a commercial crop by modern growers because a law prevents them from raising it. A treaty between the United States Government and certain Indian tribes in the Great Lakes region gives these Indians the exclusive right to harvest and market wild rice. For these tribes, it is their chief source of income.

The early Indians also developed tobacco, which they smoked in long clay pipes they called calumets and we refer to as peace pipes. Yams, cocoa, avocados, strawberries, and pineapples were other products grown by the American Indians that were unknown to the rest of the world before the coming of Columbus.

As a general rule, the Indians did not clear farms out of the forest as the white settlers did in later years. Instead, they planted their crops in natural clearings, or in areas that had been burned out by forest fires. Since they had no way of pulling up the charred stumps, they sowed their seeds in zig-zag rows around them.

Work on the farms was done by the women and older children. The men were the hunters and fighters, and they considered manual labor beneath their dignity.

Indians used scarecrows to guard their cornfields, just as farmers do today. But the Indian scarecrows were live. Old women who were too feeble for other work, or small children, sat on raised platforms in the middle of the fields to keep the crows from devouring the ripening grain.

Many Indians, especially those of the

eastern tribes, did not use their own names. They believed that if an enemy called them by their true names, he could destroy their power. The famous Chief Powhatan's real name, for example, was Wahunsonacock. Powhatan was the name of the Indian confederacy that he founded. The real name of his daughter, Pocahontas, who is renowned for saving the life of Captain John Smith, was Matoaka. Pocahontas was a nickname meaning "playful one."

The early Indians developed tobacco, which they smoked in long pipes such as the one held by the Blackfoot above. He is wearing a ceremonial shirt decorated with ermine tails.

What were the Indians' games? Although the Indian braves were usually much too busy hunting, fishing, and fighting to have time for sports, they did occasionally pass the time by playing games. In prehistoric Indian caves, archaeologists have found carved pieces of bone believed to have been used for playing a primitive version of dice. In some parts of the Southwest, the Indians played, and still play, a peculiar game for which they had no special name. It goes like this:

Two teams of four men each sit on the ground facing each other. In front of each man is a foot-high pyramid of sand. At a given signal, the men of one team turn their heads. As they do so, a member of the opposing team inserts a small stone into one of the sandpiles. The object of the game is for the first team to guess which pile of sand the stone is in. Sometimes the players bet on the outcome, but usually they play for fun.

Most of the Indian games, however, were extremely rough. Lacrosse, which is played in modern colleges in a simplified form, is a good example. The object of the game as the Indians played it was to bat a wooden or leather ball from one goal line to another with a racket. Sometimes the goals were a mile or more apart and as many as five hundred braves played on each side. The only set rule was "anything goes." Usually the surest way to keep an opposing player from getting the ball away from you was to knock him down with your racket. Broken arms and legs were common occurrences; and it was a rare game in which one or more players were not killed. As a general rule, lacrosse was played between two opposing tribes. The game was the next best thing to actual war.

Fast-running early Pueblo Indians hurl "throwing sticks" at jackrabbits, driving them towards nets raised from the ground to prevent their escape.

Sitting in their birchbark canoe, Indian women gather wild rice and flail the kernels into baskets.

With squash growing among the corn, early Indian Pueblo farmer works his "field" with a digging stick. Old women and small children served as scarecrows.

There was no baseball World Series, but lacrosse, played with special sticks and a stuffed deerskin ball, was an Indian game in which villages, and even tribes, competed.

Indians used to build stands for fishing which gave them an excellent foothold for netting salmon migrating up the river to spawn.

The Indians had many forms of wrestling. One of these, which is today called "Indian wrestling," is done with the legs only. Foot-racing over long distances was another favorite Indian sport.

Perhaps the cruelest Indian competition of all was self-torture inflicted during sun dance ceremonies of some Plains Indian tribes. It took many forms. In one of them, two or more young men held a red-hot coal under their armpits. The one who could keep it there longest was the winner. In another, a rawhide thong was threaded through the chest-muscle. The young braves vied with each other to see how long it would take them to pull it free. The scars of such ordeals were marks of honor.

The Northeastern Forest Dwellers

Broadly speaking, there were five principal groups of Indians living in what is now the United States when Columbus arrived. Of these, the most numerous were the tribes that inhabited the area between Canada on the north and Florida on the south, and from the Atlantic Ocean on the east to the Mississippi on the west.

These were the tribes that the first wave of English immigrants met when they settled the original colonies in the early seventeenth century. It was these Indians who showed the strange pale-faces from across the Big Water how to live in the great American wilderness, how to plant corn and beans, and how to fertilize each hill of corn with a dead fish to make the grain grow better. A few years later, a bitter, two hundred year long series of Indian wars began against the relentless push of the white invaders.

The domain of the eastern Indians

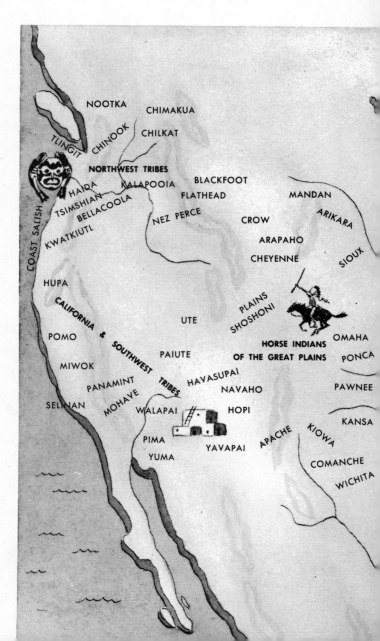

was a vast, unending virgin forest that stretched across almost half the continent. Huge trees — oaks, ashes, chestnuts, elms, sycamores, tulip trees, locusts — towered a hundred feet or more into the air. Their topmost branches often interlocked and twined together, covering the land with an infinite roof of solid greenery.

The deep woods were frightening to the first English settlers. If a man ventured more than a few feet from a forest path, he might become hopelessly lost, and wander around until he died from starvation and terror. But to the Indians, the woods were home. The Indians were as much a part of the forest as were the herds of deer, or the innumerable grouse and pigeons. The forest gave the Indians everything they needed for their simple way of life. They thought of the limitless forest as a god; they were its children. They hunted game beneath the trees, and fished in the sparkling streams.

The forest Indians lived, for the most part, along the banks of the great rivers that wound like giant snakes through the wilderness. The rivers were the roadways that they traveled in canoes made of birchbark. They sewed the bark together with the long, thin roots

Because there is no connection in aboriginal North America between language and culture, scientists have been unable to classify the American Indian by these usual ties. The Cheyenne and Crow tribes shared a common culture, but spoke languages which fell into different classifications. And there were over 1500 tribes, each with its own dialect!

Grouping into races proved just as unsatisfactory. Tribes that belonged to the same over-all race still had distinctly different cultural patterns.

The most serviceable breakdown is into regions as, in most cases, the cultural patterns of tribes living in the same region showed strong similarity. Even with this method, each expert finds divisions and subdivisions of his own. To make it as simple as possible, we have divided the tribes into: Indians of the Northeast, the Southeast, the Great Plains, the Northwest, the Southwest and California, and the Eskimos of the Far North. This very rough division still gives a workable grouping of tribes within these areas.

It wasn't until the coming of the white man that the different groups among the American Indians began to show similarity in cultures and histories.

15

Ojibwa village with bark-covered huts and tipis and birchbark canoes.

Wampum belts were used as "money" and to seal treaties and agreements. The one pictured shows an Indian and a white man (the fatter one) "making friends."

of tamarack trees, and they water-proofed the seams of their canoes with the thick, heavy resin of gum trees.

Their homes were wigwams made of strips of birchbark sewed over a frame-work of pine poles. In the winter, they made sleds of birchbark that pulled heavy loads over the snow. They invented snowshoes for walking over the deep drifts by weaving rawhide thongs over frames made of ash or hickory.

The northeastern Indians used some objects much as we use money. The shells of quahog clams were carved, strung into strands of beads, and woven into decorative belts. The Indian word for this "money" was wampumpeag. The English settlers shortened the name to wampum.

The Indians were a very clean people. In a period when Europeans sel-

dom bathed, the Indians took baths regularly. When they washed in the rivers, they rubbed their bodies with a fern that made a soapy, cleansing lather. They took steam baths in huts that were heated by pouring water over hot rocks. The Indian men did not shave. Instead, they plucked the hairs from their faces with clam shells. Indians rarely had a mustache or beard.

What were Indian towns like?

While many of the Indians of the northeast woodlands roamed as nomads through the woods, others — especially those along the Atlantic coast and around the Great Lakes — lived in towns. These towns had names, just as ours do today: Patuxet, Shawmut, Monongah, Hackensack, Waukegan, Chicago. Every town had its own chief, who, in turn, was under a tribal leader.

Each town was usually composed of domed houses shaped like modern quonset huts. They were built of stick frameworks over which strips of hide or

Iroquois mask, carved out of a living tree and worn in the ritual to ward off the "False Faces" (the evil spirits).

elm bark were laid. Some of them were large enough to house two or more families, and many had fireplaces to provide heat for cooking and warmth in winter. The chief and his family generally lived in a longhouse, several times larger than the normal dwelling, which also served as a council house and community center.

The town itself was surrounded by a high palisade of pointed logs, which gave protection against surprise raids by enemy war parties. The houses were spaced in a circle around the inside of the palisade, leaving the center of the town open for ceremonial fires, feasting, dancing, and other tribal rites.

Spread over the land outside the walled town were the cornfields, vegetable gardens, and tobacco patches.

There was one area in this vast territory

What was the "Dark and Bloody Ground"?

which was so thinly settled by the Indians that it was practically uninhabited. This was the mountainous

Indian village, protected by a palisade.

The Serpent Mound in southern Ohio, a quarter of a mile long, was an effigy, not a burial place.

At left, a carved pipe head, found in an Oklahoma mound.

forest land that now comprises the present-day state of Kentucky. No single Indian tribe claimed the region. The northern and southern tribes used it as a hunting ground, and bitter enemies as a battleground. Whenever two hunting parties from rival tribes met, they fought until one or the other was wiped out or forced to run away. So the Indians called it "Kentucky," which means "Dark and Bloody Ground." The mound builders were probably the first people to settle there.

Who were the Mound Builders? The early Indians of the Northeast, unlike the tribes of the Southwest, left very few relics behind them. The most fascinating are the mounds of earth that are found most frequently in the Ohio Valley. The earliest of these curious structures were built about two thousand years ago.

Scientists believe that when some of the wandering tribes first settled in towns and became farmers as well as hunters, they began to honor their dead instead of simply leaving the bodies behind on the trail. Apparently, they allowed the dead to accumulate over a period of perhaps ten or fifteen years. Then, when several hundred skeletons had piled up, they were all buried together in a common grave and covered over with earth.

All of the burial mounds had ceremonial forms. They were usually shaped like animals — snakes, buffaloes, deer, or bears. A few are made in the form of tusked elephants, which probably goes back to ancient tribal memories of mastodons and mammoths. In southern Ohio, the famed Serpent Mound, which represents a striking snake, is more than a quarter of a mile long. The city of Moundsville, West Virginia, was named for the many mounds that are found all around it.

About the year 1300, temple mounds spread all over the South and up the Mississippi. Flat-topped, they served as bases for temples and chief's houses. The Cahokia Mounds, near East St. Louis, Illinois, include the largest earthwork in the world, Monk's Mound.

The Indians did not understand the **Why did Indians fight the white settlers?** white settlers' overpowering need for land. To the Indian, all land was owned in common by the tribe. It was the right of every hunter to seek game wherever he pleased, and to plant his crop in available clearings.

For the most part, the Indians welcomed the first white men who came to their shores. The famous Chief Tisquantum — the English called him Squanto — showed the Pilgrims how and where to plant corn, catch fish and clams, and hunt deer and turkeys. It is doubtful if the little colony at Plymouth could have survived its first year without help. He was an honored guest at the first Thanksgiving feast.

At Jamestown, in Virginia, Chief Powhatan asked Captain John Smith,

Not all mounds were burial mounds or effigies. Some, especially in the Southeast, were bases for temples. The Indian at right is the Chief of one of the temple mound tribes.

"Why should you take by force from us that which you can obtain by love?" And he, too, like Squanto, made the foreigners welcome.

But to the English, the ownership of land was all-important. When they needed new acreage on which to plant their corn or tobacco, they simply took it from the Indians. This was especially true when tobacco became the chief cash crop of the settlers in Virginia. In both the North and the South, the Englishmen constantly extended their holdings deeper into the forest. They cut down the trees, cleared great areas for plantations, killed the game, and ruined the Indians' hunting grounds.

The Indians were bewildered by this turn of events, but at first they accepted it. Then, as was only natural, they began to resist by the only means they knew — fighting.

The first mass Indian retaliation came in 1622. Chief Opechancanough, a younger brother of Powhatan who succeeded him as Sachem of Eastern

TOBACCO
LEAF

Virginia, led a band of warriors out of the forest, struck the farms and plantations along a one hundred and forty mile front and killed three hundred and forty-seven people. The settlers fought back. And the war raged on and off for more than a decade, with hundreds of dead on the English side and thousands among the Indians. In the end, the Indians were overpowered. Opechancanough was killed, and the remaining Indians were put on reservations. This was the first in a long series of Indian retreats that would see the white man grind the proud Indian down into the dust of defeat and rule all of the New World from the Atlantic to the Pacific.

In 1637, only seventeen years after the landing of the Pilgrims, the Puritans in New England began a series of wars against the Pequot tribe, who inhabited parts of what are now Connecticut and Rhode Island. The Pequots' crime was the same as that of the Indians in Virginia; they wanted to keep their tribal hunting grounds.

Indians setting fire to a pioneer home during King Philip's War.

In a series of brutal fights in which the Puritan tactic was to take a Pequot village by surprise, burn it, and kill all the inhabitants, all but about fifty of these Indians were murdered. The few survivors were sold into slavery in Bermuda. Thus, the entire Pequot tribe ceased to exist.

One of the bloodiest of the clashes between the Indians and

Who was King Philip?

the whites in New England is known as King Philip's War. A young Indian named Metacomet was Chief of the Wampanoags, the tribe that had first befriended the Pilgrims. The English called him King Philip. As his father had done before him, Philip made every effort to get along with his white neighbors.

But the leaders of Plymouth, which in fifty years had grown enormously in population, insisted that the Wampanoags place themselves under complete subjugation to the English. In addition, they demanded that the Indians pay a yearly tribute to the colony of one hundred pounds. Philip decided to fight rather than submit.

A number of other New England tribes, including the powerful Narragansets, joined him. In the spring of 1675, Philip began making systematic attacks on New England towns and villages. The young chief demonstrated an amazing ability as a commanding general. In a little more than a year, he had attacked and damaged more than half of all the settlements in the Plymouth colony, and completely wiped out at least a dozen of them.

The Puritan soldiers, in turn, at-

Portrait of Tecumseh, the Shawnee Chief.

tacked the Indian towns, slaughtering all of their inhabitants to the last child. By 1678, the end was at hand for King Philip, and his braves.

The outcome of this war, the most destructive in New England history, was inevitable. By this time, the English colonists in New England outnumbered the Indian population by about four to one. And as would happen in all the other Indian wars of our history, the Indians were overcome by the combined weight of man and gun.

King Philip was hunted down and killed, and his wife and only son were taken to the West Indies and there sold as slaves.

By the time the Revolutionary War was

What was Tecumseh's dream?

over, there were nearly three million people living in thirteen colonies. These colonies, which were to become the original thirteen states, extended along the Atlantic Seaboard east of the Appalachian Mountain range. Although some Indian tribes had fought with the British against the Americans in the war, most of them had retreated westward across the mountains into what was generally known as the Ohio Country. In a broad sense, this took in most of what we now call the Middle West.

But when the war had been won, and the new United States had gained its freedom, people began looking toward the valley of the Ohio River as the natural area for national expansion. Daniel Boone had led the way into Kentucky, and other pioneers had done the same in the lands to the north.

A young Shawnee chief, named Tecumseh, dreamed of a great united Indian nation west of the Ohio. He determined to make the Ohio River the dividing line between the lands of the Indians and the whites. He and his twin brother, who was called the Prophet, recruited a large band of young warriors and set up headquarters at the mouth of the Tippecanoe River in what is now Indiana.

In the fall of 1811, at a time when Tecumseh was away from headquarters on a mission to enlist other Indians to his cause, an American army under General William Henry Harrison attacked the Prophet's men and routed them. As a result, the Indian army broke up into isolated segments of futile resistance, and Tecumseh's grand vision went up in black clouds of gunsmoke.

Partly on the strength of his victory at Tippecanoe, General Harrison was later elected President of the United States. Tecumseh, his dream of a united Indian state shattered, joined the British Army in the War of 1812 and was killed in battle.

Now settlers from the eastern states began pouring into the Middle West in a flood, and the defeated Indians were driven back even farther in their long, unhappy retreat into the setting sun.

Who was Black Hawk? After Tippecanoe, American settlers had streamed into practically all of Illinois, Wisconsin, and Missouri, and some were infiltrating even farther west. Then, in 1832, an old chief of the Sauk Indians, named Black Hawk, led his braves on the warpath in a last desperate effort to save his homeland. An army of militia from the border states, led by units of the American Regular Army, took to the field to stop him.

The campaign, known as Black Hawk's War, was a short one. And for the Indians, it was hopeless. Black Hawk was captured, and his people

Abnaki	Mohegan
Algonquin	Narraganset
Cayuga	Ojibwa
Delaware	Oneida
Erie	Onondaga
Huron	Pequot
Iroquois	Peoria
Kickapoo	Sauk and Fox
Massachuset	Seneca
Miami	Shawnee
Micmac	Susquehanna
Mohawk	Tuscarora

Some of the more important tribes among the North-Eastern Forest Dwellers are listed above.

were moved to a reservation in Iowa. This brief war was the last organized resistance of the Indians east of the Mississippi River.

Black Hawk's War is chiefly remembered today because a young postmaster, named Abraham Lincoln, served as a captain in the Illinois Militia.

The Southeastern Farmer Tribes

For the most part, the tribes that were native to the southeastern part of what is now the United States lived much the same as did their neighbors to the north. Yet their lives were more leisurely. The winters were mild, and the summer heat was relieved by the cooling breezes that blew over the many rivers and bayous which crisscrossed the land.

Game was as plentiful as it was in the North, and fish were even more so. The temperate climate and longer growing season made primitive agriculture easy. In fact, virtually all of the crops developed by Indian farmers had their origins in the Southeast.

These Indians traveled on the intertwining waterways in canoes made from dug-out logs. They used blowguns for hunting as well as bows and arrows. Their houses were usually made of sticks and reeds, and in swampy country, they were elevated on stilts for protection against snakes and alligators. On ceremonial occasions, the important men of the tribe wore brilliant cloaks of bird feathers. And, like their unrelated namesakes in far-off India, some wore turbans on their heads.

Because the initial waves of English settlers landed along the Atlantic coast from Virginia northward, the southern

Indians were relatively free from the encroachment of the white men until shortly before the Revolutionary War. The inevitable scattered skirmishes between Indians and whites, especially in Georgia and the Carolinas, did occur. But after the Revolutionary War was won, and an independent United States founded, Americans in the new southern states began to move west in what amounted to a mass migration.

At first, the Indians — particularly the powerful Creeks and Cherokees — made a sincere effort to adjust themselves to the English ways. They became skilled farmers and cattle-breeders. Some of the wealthier individuals owned large plantations which they worked with Negro slaves. The great Cherokee teacher, Sequoyah, devised a printed alphabet and gave his people their first written language. Many Indians learned to read the Bible and were converted to Christianity.

The new American government wanted the Indian territory that lay between the two Spanish holdings, Florida

What was Sequoyah famous for?

Standing on a notched log ladder, a Natchez Indian fills a corn crib, which is raised on a platform for protection against insects and weather.

A Yuchi village of the 18th century. The structure of the log cabins shows how Indians were influenced by contact with the white settlers.

and Louisiana, as a "buffer" state. Accordingly, the United States made a treaty with the southern Indian tribes. If the tribes would cede certain lands to the United States, the United States Government solemnly swore to guarantee the remaining boundaries of the Indian nations forever.

When Napoleon came to power in France, he forced Spain to cede Louisiana to France. Then, in 1803, needing money for his European conquests, he sold the entire Louisiana Territory to the United States for fifteen million dollars. This broke the back of Spanish power in North America. Now that Spain was no longer a menace to the infant United States, Americans began pushing westward into Indian territory in ever-increasing numbers. The Indian treaties were ignored as the white man sought more and more new fertile farmland.

When the War of 1812 broke out between the English and Americans, many of the southern Indians joined the British in protest against American seizure of their lands. These anti-American warriors were known as Red Sticks because it was their custom to declare

Seminole Indians, in a dugout canoe, pass in front of their elevated houses on the calm Everglades waters.

war by erecting a red pole in the center of their villages.

The Red Sticks raged through much of the South. At Fort Mims, in Alabama, they massacred all but a handful of the white settlers who had taken refuge there.

Who were the Seminoles?

Following the final victory over the British at the Battle of New Orleans, General Andrew Jackson moved against the Red Sticks to finish them off once and for all. Finally defeated, the Creeks fled to northern Florida. That Spanish territory had long been a refuge for scattered groups of Creek, Hitchiti, Yuchi, and Yamasee Indians who had banded together to form a new tribe called the Seminoles ("Run-away").

The Seminoles, angry to have lost yet more land and determined to keep what they had left, "took up the hatchet" against the white man in the First Seminole War. As a result, the weakened government of Spain ceded Florida to the growing United States.

Many years later, still fighting, the Seminoles were driven deep into the Everglades, finally rounded up, and their few survivors shipped to reservations in the West. The American government agreed to allow some Seminoles to remain in southern Florida, and a number of their descendants live there today.

What was the "Trail of Tears"?

After the Red Stick uprising had been quelled, there was a rising clamor to clear the Indians out of the entire southeast and move all of them, bag and baggage, west of the Mississippi. With the election of Andrew Jackson as President, in 1828, and the discovery of gold in the nation, this became our national policy. Jackson, himself a frontiersman, was the leader of the movement. Two years later, Congress passed the Indian Removal Act, and President Jackson signed it into law. It provided that all Indians must give up the rights to any lands east of

American soldiers attack a Creek village during the Creek War.

Alibamu	Creek
Apalachee	Natchez
Biloxi	Powhatan
Catawba	Seminole
Cherokee	Tuscarora
Chickasaw	Yamasee
Choctaw	Yuchi

Some of the more important Southeastern Farmer tribes are listed above.

the Mississippi. In return, they would be granted new lands in the West.

Many of the Indians, notably the Cherokees, resisted the move. But like all Indian resistances, theirs was foredoomed to failure. At last, with all hope gone, the tribes began the long trek to the Mississippi and beyond. As many as four thousand Indians died of hunger, exposure, and disease along the way. The Indians called it "the Trail of Tears."

In return for the lush lands of Alabama, Georgia, and the Carolinas, the exiled Indians were given territory on the comparatively barren plains of what is now Oklahoma. President Jackson promised that rights to this new land would endure "as long as the rivers shall run and the grass shall grow." The treaty the Indians were forced to sign said that "no part of the land granted them will ever be embraced in any Territory or State." But Oklahoma became a United States territory in 1890, and the 46th State of the Union in 1907. And the Indians were crowded even farther into the most undesirable parts of the land.

But there is one small ironic piece of poetic justice in the whole shameful Indian removal story. With the admission of white settlers to Oklahoma territory, the Indians were resettled on reservations in sections of the state that appeared to have no value at all to the Americans. Then oil was discovered on some of the reservations, and many of the tribes, who shared their wealth in common, made millions!

THE TRAIL OF TEARS.

BUFFALO HUNT

The Horse Indians of the Great Plains

It was simple for the white man to sweep the Indian out of his way in his steady migration westward from the Atlantic to the Mississippi. But once the Americans crossed the "Father of Waters," and started their wagon trains over the Great Plains, they ran into real trouble. They ran head-on into a bloody, "winner-take-all" war that was to last for fifty years!

Most of the major American Army defeats during Indian wars and uprisings were the direct result of the war waged by Indian cavalry, the world's finest.

When we think of Indians in general, usually a picture of the Plains Indian comes to mind. It is the Plains Indian that we see in movies and on television, even though he is usually unjustly cast as the villain.

How did the Plains Indians live? In order to understand the Indian wars in the West, it is necessary to know exactly how the Plains Indians lived. In the early years of the 1800's, when the white

Eastern Apache	Kiowa
Arapaho	Mandan
Arikara	Missouri
Blackfoot	Omaha
Caddo	Osage
Cheyenne	Pawnee
Comanche	Ponca
Crow	Quapaw
Dakota	Plains Shoshoni
Iowa	Sioux
Kansa	Wichita

Some important tribes of the Plains are listed above.

The Plains tribes rarely lived in towns. They followed the buffalo herds, moving their tipi villages from place to place. Here, Blackfoot Indians pitch their tipis outside a fur company's fortified trading post.

men first came into contact with them, the lives of the Plains Indians revolved around two animals — the horse and the buffalo.

The horse had evolved originally some millions of years before on these very same Great Plains. It had been hunted by the prehistoric Indians as food. Then, for some mysterious reason, after the end of the last Ice Age, it had vanished from the Western Hemisphere along with the camel and the giant hairy elephant. The first horses that the Plains Indians saw were those brought to North America by Cortez and the other Spanish conquistadors.

Most Plains tribes were nomads. But there were exceptions. The Caddo, for instance, were an agricultural tribe. They were excellent potters and had settled down in more permanent dwellings that looked like thatched beehives.

Some of these Spanish war horses escaped. Others were stolen by the Indians after they discovered the uses these strange four-legged "mystery dogs," as they called them, could be put to. And before many years had passed, the horse had completely revolutionized the In-

dians' lives. Not only did they learn to ride, they trained the horses to pull their loads.

It is an odd fact that no American Indian — not even the highly cultured Aztecs of Mexico — ever thought of the wheel. The wheel is perhaps the simplest of all mechanical devices, and is the one upon which almost all of our modern machinery is based. But somehow the idea of rolling a heavy object over the ground never occurred to an Indian. Instead, the Plains Indians used a sort of drag-sledge which was known as a travois. This consisted of two long, slender pine poles with a buffalo hide stretched between them. The load was fastened to the hide, the lower ends of the poles dragged along the ground. Originally, the travois had been pulled by big dogs, or by squaws. But the horse

Originally, the travois had been drawn by squaws or by dogs. The Spaniards introduced the Indians to the horse, and horsepower proved superior to dog or "squawpower."

proved to be a far more efficient beast of burden.

By the time the first white men from the East saw them, the Plains Indians had become perhaps the finest horsemen the world has ever known. They rode bareback, with only a single-rein hackamore noosed around the horse's muzzle. They rode like centaurs, directing their mounts only with the motions of their bodies.

The horse made the Plains Indian a formidable foe of the U.S. Army from 1860 to 1890. They were described by an American general as "the finest light cavalry in the world." Only

The Plains Indians became perhaps the finest horsemen the world has ever known. Here, a Comanche brave is shown roping a wild pony.

The "Mountain Men," dressed in Indian buckskins and moccasins, learned to live like Indians and usually got along well with them.

three times in history has a large American military force been entirely wiped out to the last man by an enemy. In

each case, those enemies were mounted Plains Indians.

The other animal basic to the life of the Plains Indian was the buffalo. In fact, the buffalo *was* the Indian's whole economic life. Apart from the few wild roots and berries that he picked, game-birds that he snared, and dishes of stewed dog that he served as a delicacy, buffalo meat was the Indian's main food. He made his clothes, his moccasins, and the covering for his tipis from its hide. He made thread and rope from its sinews, and needles and other tools from its bones. In those parts of the plains where wood was all but nonexistent, he made his fires from dried buffalo dung.

Why was the buffalo important?

Before the coming of the white invaders to the Great Plains, buffalo herds wandered over the plains in almost countless millions. Early explorers reported seeing herds that extended from horizon to horizon, covering the ground like a single moving carpet.

Unlike the Indians of the East and Pacific West, the Plains tribes rarely lived in towns. Instead, they moved their tipi villages from place to place, following the buffalo herds as they grazed across the endless grasslands. The Plains Indian had no economic problems. He hunted the buffalo from horseback, killing only as many as he needed, never making as much as the smallest dent in the teeming herds. His future seemed secure. Then the white man followed his star of destiny across the Mississippi. The Plains Indian was in his way.

The white man's trail across the western plains was littered with broken promises. The Indian had a traditional code of honor. When he gave his word, he meant it; he expected other people to do the same. But the United States Government and its representatives continually made pledges to the Indian tribes that they had no intention of keeping, as we have seen in the case of President Jackson and the Indians of the Southeast.

What caused the Plains Wars?

The first white pioneers to venture into the broad Indian lands beyond the Mississippi were hunters and trappers known as "mountain men." The western mountains were alive with all kinds of fur-bearing animals and there was a brisk market in eastern cities for all the skins that a trapper could take.

For the most part, the mountain men got along well with the Indians. Many of them lived with the tribes, married Indian wives, and adopted Indian ways. They posed no threat to the tribes' way of life, and most of the time the Indians allowed them to hunt and trap in peace.

But in the two decades before the Civil War — during which time both California and Oregon became States of the Union — a flood of emigrants began to flow westward. Half of them were headed for the gold fields of California; the rest for the rich farming country in Oregon's Willamette Valley. The grass-grown, treeless Plains were known as the "Great Basin." At that time, they were considered unfit for habitation by white men, and the emigrants hurried through them as quickly as they could.

The Indians resented this trespassing on land that the government in Washington had said belonged to them exclusively, but at first they let the travelers pass. Then as the flood of emigrant wagons became a rushing torrent, the buffalo began leaving certain parts of the Plains, ruining the tribes' sacred hunting grounds. A few scattered fights naturally followed, and a number of white men were killed.

The U. S. Army established a series of protective forts all the way across the Indian country. The Indians regarded this as a clear-cut violation of their treaties with the government, and the scattered skirmishes grew into the beginning of an all-out war.

While the Civil War was still raging in the East, President Abraham Lincoln signed two laws that—although he probably did not realize it — were destined to turn the Indian conflict into a flaming holocaust, and, in the end, wipe out the Plains Indian.

What were the Homestead and Railroad Acts?

One of these was the Homestead Act. It provided that any American citizen could stake a claim to farming land, and after working it for a certain period of time, become its legal owner. The other was the Railroad Act. This supplied government funds for building a transcontinental railroad that would connect the Atlantic and the Pacific with a ribbon of steel rails.

When the War between the States was over at last, the effect of both these laws hit the Plains Indians with full and stunning force.

Homesteaders began swarming onto the Plains, fenced them in, plowed up the grass to plant their crops, and in the process, drove the buffalo away. Cattlemen cleared out the buffalo to make room for their beef herds. And they, too, soon started fencing in huge areas of the Plains with barbed wire.

The railroads were perhaps the greatest buffalo-destroyers of all. In order to feed the thousands of construction workers, the companies hired professional buffalo hunters who slaughtered the great beasts ruthlessly. The best known of these hunters was the famous Buffalo Bill Cody. Bit by bit, the Indians found their hunting grounds shrinking, and their means of livelihood disappearing. Like all the Indian tribes in American history before them, they had no choice except to fight back.

In all justice to the white settlers, it must be said that, as individuals, most of them tried to deal fairly with the Indians. But they simply did not understand the Indians' problems, any more than the Indians understood theirs.

The East was becoming crowded; the land was being worn out. The soil of the Great Plains was rich and fertile, and the "manifest destiny" of the United States obviously lay in the West. To the homesteader of the sixties, seventies, and eighties, the broad Plains lands were going to waste. The government in Washington had said that emigrants were entitled to settle on them and bring them to fruition. The Indians, therefore, in the emigrants' minds, were cruel savages who stood in the way of progress.

Like most wars, the Plains Wars were based on mutual misunderstanding.

Famous Indian fighters. Leading military men of the period generally agreed that, man for man, the Plains Indians were the world's finest fighters. Many of their chiefs, too, developed into surprisingly able generals, often out-thinking and out-maneuvering the officers of the U.S. Army units that were sent against them. They were able to follow the movements of the American soldiers by means of smoke signals, the Indian "telegraph" system that could flash messages across hundreds of miles in a few hours.

Many of these chiefs had fascinating names that enliven the pages of history: Red Cloud, Little Big Man, Kicking Bird, Low Dog, Charging Bear, Crazy Horse, Two Moons, Spotted Tail, Black Kettle, Dull Knife, Sitting Bull, Rain-in-the-Face, Trailing-the-Enemy, Man-Afraid-of-His-Horses.

But although their names sound comical to us, there was nothing funny about the way they led their mounted braves on the warpath in defense of their homeland.

For more than thirty years, the Great Plains was a continuous battlefield. The fights flared up in unpredictable spots like scattered flashes of flame in a forest fire.

How did a cow cause a massacre? In the beginning, most white officers tended to underestimate the Indians' fighting qualities. Such carelessness led to the fate of Lt. J. L. Grattan and his men in the summer of 1854. Lt. Grattan was fresh out of West Point and had come

In the beginning, most white officers tended to under-estimate the Indian's skill in fighting. With just the bow and arrow, he was a formidable danger to the settlers. When he began to use firearms, he became a terrifying enemy, even to the white man's armies.

SIOUX CHIEF RAIN-IN-THE-FACE

to the Plains full of fight. He had only contempt for the Indians, declaring that with ten soldiers he could wipe out the entire Cheyenne tribe, and with thirty, he could chase all the Indians off the Great Plains.

His chance came when a lone Sioux shot a sick cow that had been abandoned by its emigrant owner. The Indian wanted the skin for rawhide. Although the cow was worthless, Lt. Grattan requested that he be allowed to go out and arrest the Indian. His commanding officer gave him permission, but only if he could do it without "incident or risk." Grattan at once took thirty men and two small field guns and headed for the Sioux camp.

Leaving his men outside the encampment, the lieutenant went into the village with only an interpreter by his side. There he found Chiefs Stirring Bear and Man-Afraid-of-His-Horses. The Chiefs told him that the Indian did not belong to their camp, and promised to do what they could to clear the thing up. They offered Grattan some good horses in payment for the sick cow if he would be patient and allow them to handle the matter in their own way.

Lt. Grattan refused to listen. He went back to his men and ordered them to open fire on the Indian tipis. The first volley killed Stirring Bear. At this, the Indian braves swarmed out of camp and attacked the soldiers. Grattan tried to retreat, but in doing so, he ran into a second band of Sioux. Within minutes, Grattan and all thirty of his men were dead.

This "incident" touched off a series of army raids in which several Indian villages were wiped out. The Indians, realizing now that they could not trust the white man to live up to his peace treaties, struck back with surprise raids on emigrant settlements and wagon trains. And much innocent blood began to stain the shoulder-high grass of the Great Plains.

What was the Powder River Country?

By sheer force of numbers, the Army kept continually pushing the Indian tribes farther north and west. Then, in 1865, a treaty was signed which the Indians at last decided was a good one. It gave the Sioux, the Cheyenne, the Arapaho, and related tribes all of the land between the Rocky Mountains, the Black Hills, and the Yellowstone River. This was called the Powder River Country, and was the best buffalo-hunting ground on the Plains. In addition, the Black Hills were sacred to some of the tribes as the home of their gods.

But before a year had gone by, gold was discovered in Idaho and Montana, and white prospectors were pouring into the Indian territory. And now the government in Washington attempted to negotiate a new treaty that would give the whites the right to build a trail and a series of forts through the Powder River Country. The Indian chiefs refused indignantly. But the army proceeded with the project anyway. Chief Red Cloud, of the Sioux, warned Col. Henry B. Carrington, the U.S. Commander, that "now it must be either peace or war."

Carrington ignored him and built a fort on the Little Piney River which he named Fort Phil Kearney after a noted general in the Civil War. He showed how little he knew about Indian fighting when he constructed his fort. There was open ground between the fort and its water supply. The nearest stand of timber for firewood was five miles away. Low hills all around cut off observation of the surrounding terrain.

For a while Red Cloud played a waiting game of picking off a man here and a man there, stealing occasional horses and cattle, and attacking wagon trains that came up the trail the army had made. Red Cloud even taught some of his braves a few words of English, and dressed them in captured army uniforms, so that they could approach isolated outposts and kill the soldiers on duty.

Four days before Christmas, in 1866, Red Cloud baited a masterly trap. He had quietly assembled a force of about two thousand Cheyenne, Arapaho, and Sioux, and concealed them along either side of a long narrow ridge out of sight of the fort. There, they lay in wait until the morning wood train from the fort started off for the timber. When it had gone about a mile, the train was attacked by a small party of warriors. A signalman sent back the frantic message, "Many Indians!"

A detachment of cavalry and infantry under Capt. William J. Fetterman was dispatched to the train. The captain was ordered specifically to "relieve the train, bring it in; and under no circumstances go in pursuit of the Indians."

But Red Cloud had sent out a small band of warriors to act as decoys. When Fetterman saw them appear in view, and then vanish over the ridge, he recklessly disobeyed orders and led his men after them, planning apparently to cut off the attacking party. By so doing, he ran straight into Red Cloud's ambush, and his detachment was killed to the last man.

But the Indians did not win all the pitched battles. **What was the Wagon Box Fight?** The following summer, in August, 1866, Red Cloud again decided to attack Fort Phil Kearney. What he didn't know was that the soldiers had been issued modern breech-loading rifles to replace their old muzzle loaders.

Once again, he began by attacking a wood train. But this time, the soldiers — thirty-two in all — turned over the wagons and used them as a barricade. When the two thousand or more Indians charged, they were met head-on by a withering blast of fire from the new guns that cut two-thirds of them down like stalks of wheat before a scythe. Amazed at this tremendous new fire-power, Red Cloud ordered a retreat.

However, the Wagon Box Fight turned into temporary victory for the tribes. When news of the Indians' grim determination about the Powder River Country got back to Washington, officials drew up a new treaty. By its terms, the United States promised to withdraw all forces from the Powder River. The soldiers left, the forts were abandoned, and the Indians set fire to them.

Red Cloud and the other chiefs now believed that they had won back their hunting grounds for all time. But it was not long before they realized that this treaty, too, was nothing but a wishful dream.

For the next seven or eight years, the **What was the "white man's road"?** white man's fight for control of the Plains raged on. The Powder River Country, thanks to the new treaty that followed the battles at Fort Phil Kearney, remained an isolated island in the storm that raged all around it. Tribe by tribe, the Indians were pushed out of the way.

Army detachments attacked dozens of peaceful Indian encampments, killing thousands in the process. At the Washita River, Chief Black Kettle and all of his band were massacred. Other chiefs were arrested when they went to an army camp to talk peace terms. One by one, the tribes were forced to "walk the white man's road."

Crowded into reservations in the least desirable parts of the Plains country, hunting parties were sometimes allowed to go off the reservations to kill buffalo for meat. Most of the time, however, the government gave them cattle for food. The braves frequently released the cattle on the reservation lands, and then hunted them down as they had hunted buffalo in the old days.

Now and then, restless young braves "jumped the reservation" and made bloody raids on the white settlements. Those who were not caught by army units fled to remote parts of the Plains and mountains where they managed to live as best they could.

The Apaches in Arizona, under

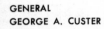

So that they wouldn't leave their wounded or dead behind, Indians on horseback often scooped up a fallen brave without dismounting or even slowing down their steeds.

CHIEF
SITTING BULL

One of the last and most famous battles in the Indian uprising against the white man became known as Custer's Last Stand.

36

The Ghost Dance was a ritual of a cult that expected it to destroy the white man, bring the Indian back into his own, and restore the buffalo to the prairie. Its followers wore a Ghost Shirt to shield them from bullets.

Chief Cochise, were tough, clever, and cruel fighters. In an effort to frighten settlers out of his territory, Cochise frequently burned white men alive when he captured them, or tortured them to death by cutting off their hands and feet by bits, or dragged them behind a running pony until dead. He murdered white families on their homesteads, and sometimes kidnapped their children.

But, in the end, the odds against him were too great, and Cochise, too, had to make peace. His people were put on reservations where they tried to learn to be peaceful farmers instead of bloodthirsty warriors.

Then, in 1874, large gold deposits were discovered in the Black Hills. By the thousands, fortune hunters began to pour into the sacred hunting grounds, which, up to now, had been worthless to the whites. But the presence of gold made a difference. It was time to break the Powder River Treaty. The government sent word to all of the chiefs that if they did not come in to the reservations, they would be considered "hostile" and would be dealt with as such by the army.

Why was the Powder River Treaty broken?

Some of the chiefs, realizing that it

was hopeless to fight against the white man's guns, came in quietly. But Sitting Bull, Chief and Big Medicine Man of the Hunkpapa Sioux, called a council of war. "The whites want war," he told the assembled chiefs. "We will give it to them."

Thousands of Sioux, Arapaho, and Cheyenne rallied around him. They included such renowned chiefs and warriors as Rain-in-the-Face, Gall, Big Road, Two Moons, Old Bear, Crow King, Spotted Eagle, Touch-the-Clouds, and Chief Crazy Horse.

In order to make big medicine, Sitting Bull ordered that one hundred cuts be made in his arms. He sat facing the sun until he fell unconscious from loss of blood. When he was revived, he proclaimed that he had had a vision. In it, he saw thousands of white soldiers coming into the Sioux camp upside down. This meant that victory was certain. The assembled chiefs decided to fight.

In the summer of 1876, a force of more than three thousand soldiers under General George Crook moved into the hills to find Sitting Bull's warriors and destroy them. One of Crook's officers was Lt. Col. George Armstrong Custer, Commander of the famed Seventh Cavalry.

Who was Long Hair?

Custer had been the swashbuckling "Boy General" of the Civil War, having rocketed to the rank of major general at the age of twenty-four, only two years after his graduation from West Point. Reduced at the war's end to the rank of captain, he was determined to regain his former glory by killing Indians. He even had dreams of becoming President of the United States. Most of the Indians called him "Long Hair," since he wore his hair at shoulder length. But the Cheyennes called him "Squaw Killer" because he had ordered the massacre of Black Kettle's people at the Washita.

As the army approached Indian country, Crook ordered Custer to take the Seventh Cavalry ahead on a scouting expedition to locate Sitting Bull's villages and on no account to attack until the balance of the soldiers came up. But when Custer located Sitting Bull at the Little Big Horn River, he saw this as his great opportunity. He sent a trooper back to report to Crook. Then he attacked!

But before he could get across the river to the Indian camp, Sitting Bull's braves, led by Rain-in-the-Face, swarmed over the Seventh Cavalry from every side. Screaming their war cry, "Hoka-hey!" — meaning "Let's go!" — the Indians cut Long Hair's men down without mercy. In half an hour, Custer and his two hundred and fifty men were dead. (See ill. p. 36.)

George Custer had wanted to go down in the history books. He did, not as a hero, but as the engineer of perhaps the worst military disaster in the annals of the U.S. Army.

Sitting Bull realized that "Custer's Last Stand" would provoke the United States into a full-scale war that the Sioux could never win. Acting not from cowardice but from a desire to protect his people, he led them across the border to safety in Canada.

The army sent more and more soldiers into the Plains country. Relent-

At left, an Arapaho Ghost Dance Shirt; at right, Chief Wovoka, the originator of the Ghost Dance cult. An illustration of the dance itself is on page 37.

lessly, the tide of white men rolled on. The Indians lost battle after battle. Their arrows and the few guns they had managed to get were no match for the rifles and cannons of the soldiers. One by one, the great chiefs came into the reservations with their people to keep them from starving.

Meanwhile, Sitting Bull and some followers had turned up in South Dakota.

1890: All of the western Indian tribes were penned up in reservations. The buffalo were gone. The warriors sat around their tipis in idleness, accepted the food doled out by the white man, did nothing except dream of the great days that had vanished.

What was the Ghost Dance?

But a few years before, a Paiute prophet, Wovoka, had had a vision. In the dream, he had been transported into Heaven. There the Great Spirit had told him that the white man would be destroyed, the Indian would come back into his own, and buffalo would again be as thick on the prairie as the stars in the Ghost Road, the Indian name for the Milky Way. But in order to do this, the Indian must support a religion that expressed itself in the Ghost Dance.

The Ghost Dance cult swept swiftly all through the West. Indians began leaving the reservations, and the U.S. Army became alarmed. One of the rituals of the Ghost Dance was the Ghost Shirt. The Indians believed that, when they were wearing this shirt, the soldiers' bullets could not harm them.

The Ghost Dance mania came to a head at Wounded Knee Creek, in the South Dakota Badlands. Sitting Bull, who had hoped it would revive the old Sioux spirit, had been arrested, and Big Foot was in command. Here, a cavalry unit rounded up several Indian bands. The soldiers started to disarm the braves, when the Indians opened fire with rifles. The cavalrymen replied with bursts from Hotchkiss guns, the forerunners of modern machine guns.

The fight was over in less time than it takes to tell about it. When the smoke had cleared, some two hundred Indians and sixty soldiers lay dead.

Wounded Knee was the last resistance of the western Indians. Their long, tragic road, at last, had come to an end.

Wovoka covered his head with a blanket to hide his shame and told his people, "My children, today I call upon you to travel a new trail. It is the only trail still open, the white man's road."

The Northwest Indians

From the standpoint of art and culture, the most advanced Indian tribes in what is now the United States were those native to the Pacific Northwest. They lived in a lush land of great natural wealth. The broad rivers that flowed to the sea teemed with salmon and other fish. The forests were filled with game and fur-bearing animals. There was no need of farming; edible plants, berries, and fruit grew in wild abundance.

A small amount of work in the spring

KWATKIUTL WOODEN
CEREMONIAL MASK.

According to Indian superstition, Tlingit medicine man shakes his rattle to drive away the evil spirits which cause the illness of a fellow tribesman.

Guests of a potlatch ceremony, some wearing masks impersonating legendary animals, arrive at a village in large richly decorated canoes. Note the many totem poles in the village.

41

and summer supplied the Indian with his needs for all year. He had much leisure time which he devoted to art.

The Northwest Indians were superb artists and craftsmen. They carved intricate ornaments and religious symbols from whalebone, walrus ivory, stone, mudstone, and wood. Their warriors often wore suits of armor, complete with visored helmet, that were made from hardwood slats. Their houses were usually built of cedar planks, and the beams and posts decorated with intricate carvings. Rich furs were used as rugs.

Their most spectacular works of art were totem poles. Carved from entire tree trunks, the fantastically designed totem poles told the history of families and clans. They also served as memorials to ancestors.

Big trees were hollowed out to make seventy foot canoes covered with artistic carvings. Two dozen men or more could put out to sea on sealing expeditions. Whales were harpooned with long lances, and then towed in to shore by the fearless Nootka.

Unlike other American Indians, the men of some Pacific Northwest tribes had hair on their faces, and sometimes sported mustaches or beards.

Most of the chiefs were extremely wealthy, and they took a childish delight in displaying their wealth.

What was a potlatch?

The richest among them owned slaves, captured from rival tribes, who usually did what little work needed to be done. Often, in order to impress visitors with the fact that his wealth meant nothing to him, the chief would order one or more of his slaves to be killed with a special club known as a "slave killer."

Another fantastic ceremony was the potlatch. One chief would invite another chief to a feast, and there heap lavish gifts upon him. In addition, the chief would bring out some of his most valuable possessions and deliberately destroy them. The visiting chief would them be compelled to give a potlatch feast in return.

The explorations of Lewis and Clark, in 1804-05, brought a swarm of American fur traders to the Northwest where they established trading posts in what is now Washington and Oregon. Forty years later, they were followed by the emigrants who wanted to homestead in the Willamette and Columbia Valleys. And wherever the white man came, the Indian was soon to depart.

Who were the Nez Percé?

One of the most powerful northwest tribes were the Nez Percé, who lived inland from the sea. They were a peace-loving people, and welcomed the white newcomers to their lands. Many of them accepted the Christian religion, and were eager to be educated in the white

Bellacoola	Kalapooia
Chilkat	Klamath
Chimakua	Kwatkiutl
Chinook	Nez Percé
Coast Salish	Nootka
Cowichan	Tlingit
Flathead	Tsimshian
Haida	Wailatpua

Some of the more important of the Northwest tribes.

Joseph, Chief of the Nez Percé, surrenders to American General Nelson Miles.

man's ways. This thirst for knowledge brought many teachers and missionaries to the northwest country. Their glowing reports, in turn, did much to bring the flood of emigrants from the East in the forties and fifties. And this swelling American population was the primary reason why the Oregon boundary dispute between the United States and Great Britain was settled in favor of the United States in 1846.

With the coming of statehood to Oregon and Washington, more settlers from the East crowded in. The army came with them for protection, and the old story of the Plains was repeated again. The white men pushed the Indians off their choicest land and took it for themselves.

Young Chief Joseph, leader of the Nez Percé, did his best to avoid an open conflict. In 1877, he reluctantly agreed to move his people to a reservation. But some of his hot-headed young braves began making raids on white settlements, and the war that Joseph had dreaded was begun. As their leader, Joseph proved himself the greatest Indian leader of them all.

Although constantly outnumbered, sometimes by as much as ten to one, he out-fought and out-thought his pursuing enemies. But he was at last overwhelmed by the numbers of the white man's army. After one last battle near the Canadian border, he was forced to surrender to the American General Nelson Miles.

Joseph went back to the reservation to die of a broken heart. The Nez Percé, and all the northwest tribes, were finished.

The Southwest and California Tribes

What was special about the Southwest and California Tribes?

When the first white hunters and prospectors explored the southwestern deserts, they found the poorest, most miserable tribes of Indians on the North American continent. These Indians lived in crude wickiup huts made of brush, and existed by hunting the sparse desert game and digging roots of desert plants from the arid soil. The white man called them "diggers."

But the Southwest Indians have a glorious past. Remnants of it can still be seen. These ancient Indians are known as the Cliff Dwellers.

They built towns of stone, that clung like eagles' nests to the rocky walls of high canyons. And, two thousand years ago, they developed a way of life that was surprisingly modern.

At that time, the dry desert country of the Southwest was much greener than it is now. There was sufficient rainfall for agriculture, and the Indians cultivated farms on the mesa flats above their cliff dwellings. There, they also pastured their flocks of domesticated turkeys, and hunted antelope and deer.

Under the overhanging walls of the cliffs, the Indians constructed stone buildings that were often three or four stories high. Most of these were "apartment houses," and some had as many as two hundred rooms. One family lived in each room. Steps chopped out of the cliff wall connected the various levels of the towns and also led up to the farms on the mesa above.

The Cliff Dwellers developed a highly organized system of industry. Some made bowls, pots, and jars from the clay in the canyon bottoms. Others wove cloth from cotton grown on the farms. Still other craftsmen made bows, arrows, knives, and hatchets.

By one of nature's curious yardsticks,

Mesa Verde cliff dwellings as they were before the drought in the late 13th century. Ruins of this greatest of all pueblos were discovered in 1888 in what is today Mesa Verde National Park in Colorado.

Pima Indians, skilled basketmakers then and today, lived in villages. They built adobe houses as well as thatched beehive huts.

Ute Indian, decked out for an ancient ceremonial dance.

Navahos today, as they were in olden times, are imaginative weavers. The child, in its typical Indian cradleboard, can be carried on mother's back. At right, Hopi pottery.

we can tell almost to the year when the civilization of the Cliff Dwellers, which had flourished for so many centuries, came to an abrupt end. This yardstick consists of the growth rings of trees. (For a more complete explanation of how this is done, see *The How & Why Wonder Book of Trees*.)

About the year 1276, more than two hundred years before Columbus landed in the New World, a great drought struck the Southwest. Crops withered and died. The grass dried up, and wild game left the area. Springs went dry and the rivers ceased to flow.

This dry period lasted for twenty-four years. During this time, the Cliff Dwellers left their fine cliffside cities and moved to other lands, which they hoped would be more hospitable. They were the ancestors of some of the desert Indians that the first explorers found.

We know today that the Cliff Dwellers were early *Pueblo* (the Spanish word for village) farmers who built their dwellings to protect themselves from hostile nomads. Pueblo culture of today, just as it was at the time the Spanish conquistadors discovered it, is characterized by its weaving, pottery- and basket-making, agriculture, and ceremonial dancing. These Pueblo Indians, among which the Zuni and the Hopi were the most important, had their cultural peak between the eleventh and fourteenth centuries. At the end of this period, nomad invaders appeared, the ancestors of a second large group of Southwest Indian tribes, the Ute, Kiowa, Western Comanche, Navaho, and Southwest Apache. (The Navaho, 80,000 in number, are believed to have more people now than they had at the time the white men came.) These nomads were hunters and seed-gatherers. A third group, which lived mainly in what is today Southwestern Arizona, devised a manner of housing very similar to the homes of the multi-family *pueblo* dwellers and those of the nomadic hunters. They were the ancestors of the Pimas. They lived in villages consisting of single dwelling houses, had some kind of agriculture, but were gatherers of wild seeds at the same time.

The Indian tribes which inhabited California had no uniform culture and no agriculture. Their common denominator was that they gathered wild seeds and nuts. Their staple foods were flour ground from acorns, nuts of the piñon tree (pine nuts), wild camas's bulbs, and berries — a diet supplemented by hunting and fishing. Washo, Pomo, Salinan, Hupa, Panamint, and Miwok are some of the California tribes.

Who are the Havasupai? When the white man first came to the desert country of the Southwest, he had little difficulty in dealing with the Indian tribes he found there. Unlike the tribes of the Great Plains, they usually found themselves better off after he came. But there is one Indian tribe that the influence of the white man has touched only lightly.

The tribe is the Havasupai. For untold centuries, they have lived in a remote corner of the floor of the Grand Canyon in Arizona. Their little isolated segment of land, watered by the Colorado River and its canyon tributaries, is rich and green. Their crops and their cattle thrive. As they have always done, they live in peace and prosperity.

Why didn't the white man want their land? The answer is simple. It was and still is too hard to reach. The canyon walls that tower above it are a mile high, and almost as sheer as the sides of a New York City skyscraper. Narrow, twisting trails wind down to the canyon floor. Many of the Havasupai have never been up to the canyon rim. The territory is part of Grand Canyon National Park.

It is gratifying to know that at least one North American Indian tribe lives today as its ancestors did.

Western Apache	Panamint
Havasupai	Pima
Hopi	Pomo
Hupa	Selinan
Maidu	Ute
Miwok	Walapai
Mohave	Yavapai
Navaho	Yuma
Paiute	Zuni

Some important Southwest and California tribes.

The "Raw Meat Eaters"

Are the Eskimos Indians? Anthropologists do not regard the Eskimos of the far north as true Indians. They look more Mongoloid (the chief Asiatic race) than do the Indian tribes that live farther south; and their language is more closely related to that of primitive Asia. It is believed that the Eskimos were the last of the emigrants to wander over the ice from Siberia. Even today, Eskimos often travel freely across the narrow Bering Strait that separates Siberia from Alaska.

The name Eskimo means "eaters of raw meat." It was given to them by the northern Indians in Canada because the Eskimo diet consisted solely of whale blubber, seal, fish, and reindeer — all of which they ate without cooking. North American Eskimos call themselves *Innuit,* and Siberian Eskimos say *Yuit.* Both words mean *men.*

Eskimos are shorter than Indians. For the most part, they have sturdy heavy-set bodies, round chubby faces, and are generally fat as a natural protection against the severe Arctic cold.

The Eskimos live very much today as they did before the first white man ventured into their ice-locked land. They make their clothing from the hides of seals and reindeer, and their boots from sealskin. Linings fashioned from the dried intestines of walruses make these garments waterproof and windproof.

In the long, cold winters, the Eskimo lives in a hut built of driftwood or whalebone, or a combination of both. For insulation, it is usually covered over with skins, stones, and snow. During the short summer, he erects a reindeer-skin tent that somewhat resembles that of his Indian neighbors to the south.

When winter's frigid cold freezes the ice far out to sea, the Eskimo sometimes hunts and fishes through holes in the ice. A hunter will stand motionless for hours at a seal's breathing hole, his spear ready. When the seal comes up for air, the hunter quickly harpoons it.

In summer, the Eskimo goes to sea in a light, sealskin-covered canoe called a *kayak.* He virtually puts this one-man boat on like a piece of clothing. When he laces himself into it, he can turn over in the water without getting wet. With his double-bladed paddle, a kayaker can quickly right himself when a wave or a gust of wind capsizes him. Whaling parties go out — often beyond the sight of land — in large skin-covered boats called *umiaks.* Sometimes the umiak is rigged with a small sail made of skins or woven grass.

Although he does most of his hunting along the seashore, the Eskimo also makes long hunting trips inland. He travels by himself, or with a single partner, and uses a dog sled for transportation over the snow. When it is time to sleep, he builds a small igloo out of snow blocks. This keeps him snug and warm. His dogs burrow under the snow.

It has been estimated that there are about fifty thousand Eskimos in all who occupy a territory extending about four thousand miles from the Aleutian Islands of Alaska to Greenland. Thus, they are the most scattered people on earth.

Cutaway view of a snow house of the Polar Eskimos, and Greenland Eskimos in front of their summer tent of skin.